ROCK RIFFS

for Trumpet

ISBN 978-1-4234-6211-8

HAL•LEONARD®
CORPORATION

7777 W. BLUEMOUND RD. P.O. BOX 13819 MILWAUKEE, WI 53213

Visit Hal Leonard Online at
www.halleonard.com

CONTENTS

Ain't Talkin' 'Bout Love
Words and Music by David Lee Roth, Edward Van Halen, Alex Van Halen and Michael Anthony

Artist: Van Halen
Album: *Van Halen*
Year: 1978

Trivia: "Ain't Talkin' 'Bout Love" was one of the few David Lee Roth-era Van Halen songs that his successor Sammy Hagar was willing to perform live when he joined the band in the mid 1980s.

Aqualung
Music by Ian Anderson
Lyrics by Jennie Anderson

Artist: Jethro Tull
Album: *Aqualung*
Year: 1971

Trivia: Ian Anderson's then-wife Jennie took the photograph of a homeless person that influenced both the lyrics to this song and the *Aqualung* album cover.

Carry On Wayward Son
Words and Music by Kerry Livgren

Artist: Kansas
Album: *Leftoverture*
Year: 1976

Trivia: "Carry On Wayward Son" was a last-minute addition to the *Leftoverture* album. The album was written and ready to record, but the rest of the band didn't want to work on any additional material. Luckily they changed their minds as soon as they heard the song.

Another One Bites the Dust
Words and Music by John Deacon

Moderate Rock ♩ = 110

Artist: Queen
Album: *The Game*
Year: 1980

Trivia: Though this was Queen's highest-charting single in the U.S., topping the Pop and even R&B charts, it appears on the list of songs compiled by Clear Channel Communications and its subsidiaries of songs that contain lyrics which may be unsuitable for airplay after the September 11, 2001 attacks.

Back in Black
Words and Music by Angus Young, Malcolm Young and Brian Johnson

Moderate Rock ♩ = 92

Artist: AC/DC
Album: *Back in Black*
Year: 1980

Trivia: This hit song from the album of the same title was the first to feature new singer Brian Johnson after the death of original front man, Bon Scott in 1980.

Track 5

Barracuda

Words and Music by Nancy Wilson, Ann Wilson, Michael Derosier and Roger Fisher

Moderately fast Rock ♩ = 132

Artist: Heart
Album: *Little Queen*
Year: 1977

Trivia: The lyrics for this song were based on the negative (but not necessarily true) press the Wilson sisters received after the relationship with their first record label went sour.

Track 12

I Feel Fine

Words and Music by John Lennon and Paul McCartney

Fast ♩ = 182
Half-Time Feel

* Chord symbols reflect implied tonality.

Artist: The Beatles
Album: *Beatles '65*
Year: 1964

Trivia: The original recording of this song was the very first to use guitar feedback.

Crazy Train
Words and Music by Ozzy Osbourne, Randy Rhoads and Bob Daisley

Artist: Ozzy Osbourne
Album: *Blizzard of Ozz*
Year: 1981

Trivia: The opening riff for "Crazy Train" is popular in professional sports, as it is the walk-up music for numerous baseball players and the introduction song for the New England Patriots football team.

Track 8

Day Tripper
Words and Music by John Lennon and Paul McCartney

Artist: The Beatles
Album: *Yesterday…And Today*
Year: 1966

Trivia: Not only has "Day Tripper" been covered numerous times, but the riff to this #5 hit has been used by Devo and 2 Live Crew on their "The 4th Dimension" and "Fraternity Record" tracks, respectively.

Track 9

Eye of the Tiger
Theme from ROCKY III
Words and Music by Frank Sullivan and Jim Peterik

Artist: Survivor
Album: *Eye of the Tiger*
Year: 1982

Trivia: Sylvester Stallone personally called Survivor's main songwriters, Frankie Sullivan and Jim Peterik, asking them to write the theme song to the *Rocky III* film after the record label's president played Stallone some tracks off the band's *Premonition* album. It was the #1 song of 1982.

Track 10

Frankenstein
By Edgar Winter

Artist: Edgar Winter Group
Album: *They Only Come Out at Night*
Year: 1972

Trivia: Edgar Winter originally played drums on this song with brother Johnny Winter's trio. They called it "Double Drum Song" and it had no keyboards in it until the synthesizer made its way into the rock scene.

Track 11

Godzilla
Words and Music by Donald Roeser

Artist: Blue Öyster Cult
Album: *Spectres*
Year: 1977

Trivia: This song, along with two other Blue Öyster Cult songs ("Fire of Unknown Origin" and "Burnin' for You") and the band's "Cross of Questioning" logo was featured on the WB network series *Supernatural*.

Track 13

Iron Man
Words and Music by Frank Iommi, John Osbourne, William Ward and Terence Butler

Artist: Black Sabbath
Album: *Paranoid*
Year: 1971

Trivia: This song, which received a belated Grammy award in 2000 for Best Metal Performance (*Reunion* live album version), appears in the video game *Guitar Hero*. The riff appears on the Xbox game *Forza Motorsport*.

Track 14

The Joker

Words and Music by Steve Miller, Eddie Curtis and Ahmet Ertegun

Moderately Slow ♩ = 88

Artist: Steve Miller Band
Album: *The Joker*
Year: 1973

Trivia: Some lyrics in this song refer to earlier Steve Miller songs ("Space Cowboy" and "Gangster of Love," for example), but there is a fair amount of controversy over the lyric "the pompatus of love." Miller claims he made the word up, however, a similar word (puppetutes) occurs in a 1954 Medallions song called "The Letter" ("discuss the puppetutes of love.") The word is also pondered in the 1996 film *The Pompatus of Love* starring Jon Cryer.

Track 17

Message in a Bottle

Music and Lyrics by Sting

Moderately Fast ♩ = 150

Artist: The Police
Album: *Regatta de Blanc*
Year: 1979

Trivia: As Sting became more famous, his relationship with drummer Stewart Copeland began to deteriorate. However, both Copeland and guitarist Andy Summers were invited to Sting's wedding in 1992, where after much pressure from the guests they performed this song, along with their hit "Roxanne."

Track 18

Money

Words and Music by Roger Waters

Moderate Rock ♩ = 120

Artist: Pink Floyd
Album: *Dark Side of the Moon*
Year: 1976

Trivia: This song, written in Roger Waters's garden, is the only song in 7/4 time to hit the top 20 in the U.S.

La Grange

Words and Music by Billy F Gibbons, Dusty Hill and Frank Lee Beard

Moderately Fast Shuffle ♩ = 160

* Chord symbols reflect basic harmony.

Artist: ZZ Top
Album: *Tres Hombres*
Year: 1973

Trivia: This song is about the Texas Chicken Ranch: the brothel on which the film *The Best Little Whorehouse in Texas* is based.

Layla

Words and Music by Eric Clapton and Jim Gordon

Moderately ♩ = 116

Artist: Derek and the Dominos
Album: *Layla and Other Assorted Love Songs*
Year: 1970

Trivia: This song's title comes from a Persian love story called *Layla and Majnun*, and was inspired by Clapton's unrequited love for George Harrison's first wife, Pattie Boyd.

Track 19

Oh, Pretty Woman
Words and Music by Roy Orbison and Bill Dees

Artist: Roy Orbison
Album: *Orbisongs*
Year: 1965

Trivia: In 1989, controversial rap group 2 Live Crew sampled a portion of this song for a parody song called "Pretty Woman." The group's management requested a license from the song's publisher but was denied. However, 2 Live Crew recorded their parody anyway. The publisher sued for copyright infringement and unfair use, and the case was heard by the U.S. Supreme Court. The Court ruled in favor of 2 Live Crew, and stated that a for-profit parody may be protected under fair use law.

Track 20

Owner of a Lonely Heart
Words and Music by Trevor Horn, Jon Anderson, Trevor Rabin and Chris Squire

Artist: Yes
Album: *90125*
Year: 1983

Trivia: This song was Yes' highest charting hit, reaching #1 in the U.S. The album *90125* introduced a new updated sound for this classic progressive rock band.

Track 21

Proud Mary
Words and Music by John Fogerty

Artist: Creedence Clearwater Revival
Album: *Bayou Country*
Year: 1969

Trivia: Written on a steamboat called the "Mary Elizabeth," this song became the band's first top 10 hit on the U.S. Pop charts. Over the years, it has been covered by a wide variety of artists, including Elvis Presley and actor Leonard Nimoy.

Refugee
Words and Music by Tom Petty and Mike Campbell

Moderate Rock ♩ = 116

Am   C5   G

Artist: Tom Petty &
The Heartbreakers
Album: *Damn the Torpedoes*
Year: 1979

Trivia: Roughly six months before the release of "Refugee" as a single, Tom Petty had to file for bankruptcy. However, the *Damn the Torpedoes* album would prove to be his breakthrough hit.

Rock You Like a Hurricane
Words and Music by Herman Rarebell, Klaus Meine and Rudolf Schenker

Moderate Rock ♩ = 124

F#5   A5   B5   D5   E5

Artist: Scorpions
Album: *Love at First Sting*
Year: 1984

Trivia: It took twelve years for the Scorpions to break the U.S. top 40 chart, which they did thanks to this 1984 single.

Smells Like Teen Spirit
Words and Music by Kurt Cobain, Krist Novoselic and Dave Grohl

Driving Rock ♩ = 116

Gsus4   C   A/B   B♭sus4   E♭   A/B

Artist: Nirvana
Album: *Nevermind*
Year: 1991

Trivia: Kurt Cobain got this song's unusual title when the phrase "Kurt Smells Like Teen Spirit" was spray painted on his wall by a friend. However, Kurt claimed he didn't know Teen Spirit was a deodorant brand name and regretted naming a commercial product in the song's title.

Track 25

Smoke on the Water
Words and Music by Ritchie Blackmore, Ian Gillan, Roger Glover, Jon Lord and Ian Paice

Artist: Deep Purple
Album: *Machine Head*
Year: 1972

Trivia: The lyrics to this song quite literally tell the story of an incident at the Montreaux Casino in Montreaux, Switzerland where a fire broke out at a Frank Zappa and the Mothers of Invention concert. Deep Purple had planned on recording the *Machine Head* album at the casino, but after the fire needed to scout out a new location, the first of which was a theater called The Pavilion. However, "Smoke on the Water" was the only song recorded at the theater because the neighbors complained about the noise.

Track 26

Stayin' Alive
from the Motion Picture SATURDAY NIGHT FEVER
Words and Music by Barry Gibb, Robin Gibb and Maurice Gibb

Artist: The Bee Gees
Album: *Saturday Night Fever*
Year: 1977

Trivia: Besides the hugely successful *Saturday Night Fever* film, this song appears on the soundtracks for *Neighbors, Airplane!, Staying Alive* (the sequel to *Saturday Night Fever*), *Cadillac Man, Honey, I Blew Up the Kid, Bushwacked, Grumpier Old Men*, and *A Night at the Roxbury*. However, only the *Saturday Night Fever* soundtrack can boast that it is the best-selling soundtrack of all time in worldwide sales.

Track 27

Sunshine of Your Love
Words and Music by Jack Bruce, Pete Brown and Eric Clapton

Artist: Cream
Album: *Disraeli Gears*
Year: 1967

Trivia: Some lyrical origins of the song are quite literal: during the writing of the song bassist Jack Bruce played this unforgettable riff at 5:00 am, while drummer Pete Brown was looking out the window awaiting the sunrise.

Sweet Home Alabama

Words and Music by Ronnie Van Zant, Ed King and Gary Rossington

Artist: Lynyrd Skynrd
Album: *Second Helping*
Year: 1974

Trivia: The many films in which this song has been featured include *8 Mile*, *Forrest Gump*, the remake of *The Texas Chainsaw Massacre*, and of course the 2002 movie of the same name (where pop singer Jewel performed it for the soundtrack). It is also the opening theme music for the NASCAR series of video games, and is played at least once during the broadcasts of NASCAR's Nextel Cup races in Talladega, Alabama.

You Really Got Me

Words and Music by Ray Davies

Artist: The Kinks
Album: *You Really Got Me*
Year: 1964

Trivia: The Kinks' record company almost didn't allow the recording of this #7 hit, whose groundbreaking guitar tone was achieved by Dave Davies slicing the surface of the speaker cone in his amplifier with a razor blade.

Walk This Way

Words and Music by Steven Tyler and Joe Perry

Artist: Aerosmith
Album: *Toys in the Attic*
Year: 1975

Trivia: The title of this #10 (1976) and #4 (1986) hit was inspired by a line spoken by the character Igor in the 1974 film *Young Frankenstein*.